The Knight Who Couldn't See Where He Was Going

Stafford Junior School

Level 9 – Gold

Helpful Hints for Reading at Home

The graphemes (written letters) and phonemes (units of sound) used throughout this series are aligned with Letters and Sounds. This offers a consistent approach to learning whether reading at home or in the classroom.

HERE ARE SOME COMMON WORDS THAT YOUR CHILD MIGHT FIND TRICKY:

water	where	would	know	thought	through	couldn't
laughed	eyes	once	we're	school	can't	our

TOP TIPS FOR HELPING YOUR CHILD TO READ:

- Encourage your child to read aloud as well as silently to themselves.
- Allow your child time to absorb the text and make comments.
- Ask simple questions about the text to assess understanding.
- Encourage your child to clarify the meaning of new vocabulary.

This book focuses on developing independence, fluency and comprehension. It is a gold level 9 book band.

The Knight
Who Couldn't See Where He Was Going

Written by
Charis Mather

Illustrated by
Eidvilė Viktorija Buožytė

Chapter One

Nothing ever happened at Castle Caligatus. Most days, the guards sat around eating food and kicking around a helmet to keep entertained. So, when the castle alarm actually sounded one morning, the last thing the guards were expecting was to have to drop their lunches and chase after a thief.

"Get up, you lot! There's a thief getting away with the king's gold!" called a guard from the watchtower. The castle guards rushed to pick up their swords and find the thief, but they were all too slow. The thief had slipped through the gates.

While the castle guards were still running to collect their helmets and swords, one splendid knight burst through the gates, his own sword in hand. Sir Noble was ready for a chase. "Come here, scoundrel," bellowed the knight. "You're not getting away from me!"

Sir Noble raced after the thief and chased him down a narrow alleyway. Just as he caught up, the clever thief kicked over a soapy bucket, spilling it in the knight's path. Unable to stop his fancy, polished boots from slipping on the slick stones, Sir Noble skidded face-first into a wall with a terrible crash.

The knight jumped to his feet, but quickly realised that his helmet's visor had jammed over his eyes. The metal was so twisted and dented that he could barely see anything except shadows and shapes. Sir Noble tugged at the ruined helmet to get it off, but it was well and truly stuck.

Sir Noble felt his way down the alley into the busy marketplace where his horse was waiting for him. "Has anybody seen a thief run through here?" he shouted into the crowd.

"Thief ran that way," someone called.
"Where?" he demanded, unable to see where they were pointing.
"To Percival's Preenary, Sir Noble," they replied.

Determined to catch the thief, the blind knight charged towards the stall. There was a CRASH as Sir Noble accidentally steered his horse into a flower stand, then a crate of plums. He finally spotted something person-shaped through his twisted helmet.

"You there! Are you the thief? I can't see a thing though this visor."

The thief was trapped in Percival's Preenary. "Oh no, not me," said the thief. "I'm... I'm Keith! Not a thief. The real thief ran over there."

"Prove it," Sir Noble challenged.

The thief thought quickly. "Sir Noble, if you remember, the thief does not have a moustache – I do," he lied.

"I'm sure you are trustworthy, Keith," he said. "But I must feel your moustache to be sure."

Keith snatched a soft hairbrush from the shelf and held it under his nose. Sir Noble reached out to feel it.

"Hmm..."
"What a fine moustache you have!"

The thief had an idea. "Sir Noble, since you can't see, why don't I guide you?"

"An excellent idea," the knight agreed. "Lead on."

Chapter Two

The knight and the clever thief began their trip. Once the excitement of the chase had worn off, the knight's new guide noticed how heavy his bag of stolen gold was. The thief had another cunning idea.

Every few steps, he slipped a handful of gold into the horse's saddlebags. When the gold was all stashed away, the thief also snuck in as many heavy rocks as he could find.

"How strange," said the knight. "My horse feels much slower than usual. It must be tired from the chase."

"It does look very tired, Sir Noble," the thief agreed.

"Why don't we stop and let the horse rest?" the thief suggested. "I know a stable just ahead where it can stay."

"What a good idea, Keith. We'll never catch up to the thief at this speed," replied the knight.

'Keith' led Sir Noble to a small house with a straw roof.

"Ah, this must be a fine stable," the blinded knight said. "I can already smell the golden straw."

The thief smiled to himself. This was not a stable at all – it was his house. And now, this was his horse!

They carried on. The knight clanked with every step. As they went, the thief did his best to lead Sir Noble into every muddy puddle he could find.

"Not another puddle!" Sir Noble cried. "I just polished my boots this morning, and now they are all muddy and wet."

"That is terrible," said the thief, eyeing the knight's expensive boots. "Why don't we swap shoes after this muddy bit? Mine are still clean and dry."

Sir Noble agreed, and they swapped their shoes. The thief wriggled his toes happily in his new, expensive boots.

As the day went on, 'Keith' led Sir Noble farther and farther away from the village. They kept walking until the thief's stomach began to rumble.

"Is that a grumbling belly I hear?" said the knight. "We should stop to eat. I always keep a spare snack with me. It's hungry work hunting criminals."

"I suppose since your helmet is stuck, I'll have to eat it all," said the thief. He licked his lips.

"Oh," Sir Noble said sadly. "I didn't think of that. Well... I suppose so."

The hungry thief couldn't have been more happy to tuck in.

Chapter Three

It had been a good day for the thief. Today, he had managed to steal a big bag of gold from the castle, a horse, some shiny boots and a delicious snack to top it all off. Sir Noble still hadn't figured out that Keith was the man they were searching for. It was about time that he found out.

The thief looked around to double-check that they were far enough away from the village.

"I've just had a thought, Sir Noble. Do you think we could get that helmet off together?" he asked.

"Maybe," the knight said. "It's worth a try."

Together, the two tugged at the dented helmet. They pushed, pulled, twisted and wiggled the battered helmet. At last, the helmet flew off with a pop.

Sir Noble was so excited about finally being able to see again that he didn't notice his companion at first. A moment later, though, Sir Noble rubbed his eyes in disbelief.

"Wait a minute... where's your moustache, Keith?"

"Ha ha!" 'Keith' laughed. "That moustache wasn't even real."

"It's you... you're the thief! It was you all along!" the knight spluttered.

"You'll never catch me now!" the thief shouted behind him as he bolted away.

The thief was right. As fast as Sir Noble ran, he couldn't keep up. Sir Noble's armour was very heavy, and he didn't have his horse to carry him. He was hungry, too, and very lost. He kept getting stones in his shoes because of the holes.

The knight stopped at a crossroads. He had no idea which way the thief had run. Until... Could that be? The knight peered closely at the footprints in the mud. "A-hah!" he said out loud. "Footprints with the royal seal – those could only be from my boots."

The knight followed the footprints to a small house with a familiar horse outside. Sir Noble kicked down the door to see the escaped thief counting out piles of stolen gold coins.

"You're under arrest, Keith the thief," said the knight triumphantly. "I might not have been able to see where I was going all day, but I think we can both see exactly where you are going now."

"... the bank?" the thief replied hopefully.

"I'll be the one going to the bank," Sir Noble said, grinning. "You are most definitely going to jail."

The Knight Who Couldn't See Where He Was Going

1. What was the fake name the thief used?

    a) Ken

    b) Kyle

    c) Keith

2. What did the thief steal? Can you remember each item?

3. Why would somebody steal something? Is it good or bad to steal?

4. Where is the thief going to be sent at the end of the story?

5. If you had to catch a thief, how would you do it?

©2022 **BookLife Publishing Ltd.**
King's Lynn, Norfolk, PE30 4LS, UK

ISBN 978-1-80155-805-1

All rights reserved. Printed in Poland.
A catalogue record for this book is available from the British Library.

The Knight Who Couldn't See Where He Was Going
Written by Charis Mather
Illustrated by Eidvilė Viktorija Buožytė

An Introduction to BookLife Readers…

Our Readers have been specifically created in line with the London Institute of Education's approach to book banding and are phonetically decodable and ordered to support each phase of Letters and Sounds.

Each book has been created to provide the best possible reading and learning experience. Our aim is to share our love of books with children, providing both emerging readers and prolific page-turners with beautiful books that are guaranteed to provoke interest and learning, regardless of ability.

BOOK BAND GRADED using the Institute of Education's approach to levelling.

PHONETICALLY DECODABLE supporting each phase of Letters and Sounds.

EXERCISES AND QUESTIONS to offer reinforcement and to ascertain comprehension.

BEAUTIFULLY ILLUSTRATED to inspire and provoke engagement, providing a variety of styles for the reader to enjoy whilst reading through the series.

AUTHOR INSIGHT:
CHARIS MATHER

Charis Mather is a children's author at BookLife Publishing who has a love for writing stories. Charis enjoys both reading and writing about the weird and wonderful, whether from the real world or from the imagination. Her studies in linguistics and experiences working with young readers have given her a knack for writing material that suits a range of ages and skill levels. Charis is passionate about producing books that emphasise the fun in reading and is convinced that no matter how much you already know, there is always something new to learn.

This book focuses on developing independence, fluency and comprehension. It is a gold level 9 book band.